Creative Lettering for Kids

Creative Lettering for Kids

Techniques and Tips from Top Artists

Jenny Doh

STERLING CHILDREN'S BOOKS

New York

STERLING CHILDREN'S BOOKS
New York

An Imprint of Sterling Publishing Co., Inc.
1166 Avenue of the Americas
New York, NY 10036

ISBN 978-1-4549-2005-2

Distributed in Canada by Sterling Publishing
c/o Canadian Manda Group, 664 Annette Street
Toronto, Ontario, Canada M6S 2C8
Distributed in the United Kingdom by GMC Distribution Services
Castle Place, 166 High Street, Lewes, East Sussex, England BN7 1XU
Distributed in Australia by NewSouth Books
45 Beach Street, Coogee, NSW 2034, Australia

For information about custom editions, special sales, and premium and corporate purchases, please contact Sterling Special Sales at 800-805-5489 or specialsales@sterlingpublishing.com.

Manufactured in China
Lot #:
2 4 6 8 10 9 7 5 3 1
10/16

www.sterlingpublishing.com

Contents

Basics

At the heart of creative lettering is something we're all familiar with—letters! As early as we can remember we're taught to write all the letters of the alphabet, in both uppercase and lowercase form. This foundation is exactly why creative lettering projects are perfect for kids. There's no need to be able to draw complicated figures or work with advanced artistic techniques to create fun, happy, and bright lettering projects.

In this book, you'll see a wide variety of lettering styles, from thick block letters to thin curly letters and everything in between. The lettering styles and different alphabets are certainly meant to inspire you, but remember that when you're actually creating, the letters will probably look at least slightly different than the ones seen on these pages. And that's okay! In fact, that's exactly how it should be. The projects in this book are a great opportunity to practice letters, document the kinds of letters you are making now, and decorate and embellish those letters using lots of fun doodling and crafting techniques.

As you're working through the projects in this book, here are a few things to keep in mind that will make each project easy-to-understand and achievable.

Tools and Materials

Each project in this book will include a list of tools and materials used by the artist, but don't feel like you have to use the same materials as the artists did. Use your imagination and what you have on hand to really make the projects your very own. Here are some general terms to acquaint you with the tools and materials used by the artists.

Acrylic Paint: Fast-drying, water-based paint that dries opaque and quickly, with results that can resemble watercolor or oil paint.

Craft Knife: This metal knife has a razor-sharp blade that can be replaced when dull. When using it to cut paper, use a metal ruler and be very careful where you put your fingers. If you need to use this tool, ask an adult for help!

Gel Pen: This pen has water-based ink that tends to be thick and opaque, resulting in rich pigments on the page. These pens also come in white, which show up clearly on dark paper, and in a variety of metallic colors.

Gouache: A form of watercolor paint that is opaque rather than transparent.

Ink: Ink comes in many colors, forms, and thicknesses. It can be permanent or water-soluble, and it can be applied as a spray or with a pen or a brush.

Light Box: Contains a backlit piece of glass or acrylic glass, and is often used by artists for tracing.

Paint Pens: These pens or markers write just like a normal pen, but use paint as the material instead of ink.

Paper: Paper comes in a variety of weights, from thin printer paper to heavyweight paper such as cardstock. Artists may suggest which weight to use if it is pertinent to the project in this book. Paper also comes in a variety of colors, even black. When working with black paper, keep in mind that not all inks will show up as clearly as you may like; gravitate toward white and metallic gel pens or bright white paint pens for black paper.

Permanent Markers: Markers with fast-drying, permanent results. If you'd like to make sure the permanent colors are right where you'd like them to be, you can always write or draw first in pencil, trace over the pencil with permanent markers, and then erase the pencil marks once the marker is dry.

Watercolor Paint: Paint made with pigments suspended in a water-soluble medium; when dry, the colors are transparent and can reactivate with water.

Techniques

The projects featured in this book will be outlined in steps by the artists, but there are a few techniques that are good to know before you get started.

Tracing: Tracing is a great method if you'd like to practice or sketch your letters with pencil before finalizing them. Once you're happy with your sketched project, place a piece of translucent paper or printer paper on top of the sketched project and use masking or washi tape to secure the layers onto a light box or well-lit window before tracing.

Carving: Carving rubber stamps or even potatoes works really well if you'd like to be able to create the same word or phrase several times, to make several different gift tags or cards for example. First, sketch the letters on your rubber block, potato, or large eraser. Keep in mind that the raised portion of the stamp is what's going to show up, so you will carve around the major outlines of each letter. For rubber blocks or erasers you will have to use a linoleum cutter or sharp craft knife, and with potatoes all you'll need is basic table utensils, including a paring knife to cut the potato in half and then a spoon to carve out the portions of the potato you don't want. Make sure a parent is supervising when you are using carving tools.

As you're finishing, adhere ink to the stamp and press it on a scratch piece of paper. This will allow you to see the stamp in action, which will point out areas that may need closer carves.

Stitching: A few of the projects in this book teach you how to stitch a fun word or phrase on a piece of paper. For these projects, keep in mind that a running stitch is created by running the needle and thread up and back down through the substrate. The backstitch is created using a running stitch, but sewn in the opposite direction of a traditional running stitch.

Creative Lettering

The projects in this book vary in necessary skills and techniques used. Some projects may work really well to do all on your own, while others may require adults to be more hands-on and helpful. Whether you work by yourself, with friends, or with adult supervision, make sure you are safe when using the tools and materials and most of all, have lots of fun!

Sarah Ahearn Bellemare

www.sarahearn.com

I have a very clear memory of sitting in the emergency room waiting to be seen for an ear infection as an 8-year-old, and my mom pulling out a pen and scrap paper from her purse to distract me. In that moment, she showed me how to write my name, letter by letter, in cursive. I had always loved my mom and grandmother's flowing, cursive handwriting, which before that day had seemed like a magical language I'd never be able to understand. In that moment, learning cursive in the emergency waiting room, it was like a whole new world was opening up to me. I've been practicing and playing with my handwriting style ever since!

favorite letter

My favorite letter is "A." It's the first letter of my last name, the first letter of my daughter's name, the first letter of the alphabet song that I've sung over and over to my babies, and the first letter my daughter learned to write. Plus, I love how the uppercase and lowercase versions of the letter look together, written out as "Aa."

favorite lettering instruments

I always have my simple sketchbook and a pencil or pen in my bag, so I'm ready to pull it out at any moment. I really like Micron-style pens and Staedtler brand pencils, both in various sizes.

lettering lesson

Polka Dot Plaque

To create this darling plaque, use washi tape to form letter shapes. Have lots of fun adding polka dots with paints, using stencils, and painting the pre-made wooden plaque.

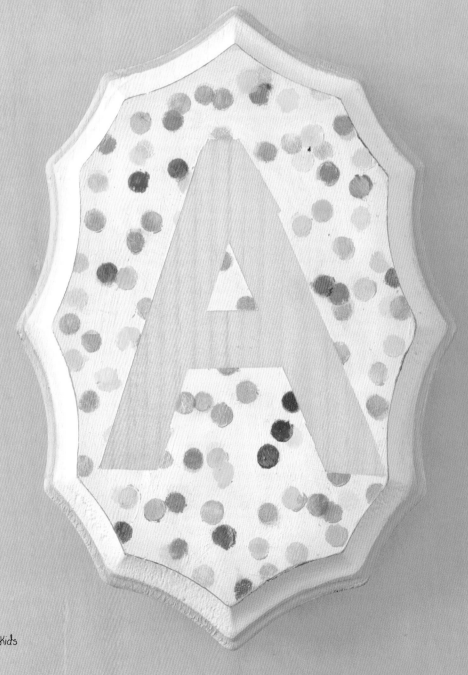

figure A

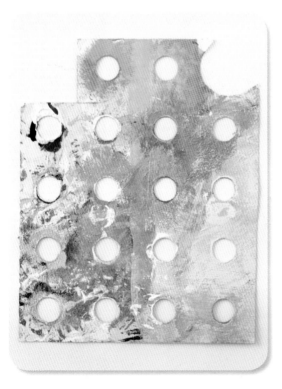

What You'll Need

* Washi tape
* Scissors
* Wooden plaque
* Acrylic paint in white and other assorted colors
* Reinforcement sticker sheet for hole-punched paper
* Small paintbrushes

Method

1 Adhere washi tape to the wooden plaque in the shape of the first letter of your name. Cut the tape at the ends on angles to make curves. Be sure the tape is very flat and secured to the boards, especially on the edges so the paint won't leak through. Rub the tape down with fingers to be sure it is smoothly and tightly adhered (fig. A).

2 Apply white acrylic paint over the entire plaque, including the portion covered by washi tape. Let dry at least 1 hour.

3 Use the backing of the Reinforcement sticker sheet for hole-punched paper as a stencil to create the polka dot background. Hold the sticker sheet securely over the plaque, and apply various colors of paint using a paintbrush. Move the sticker sheet slightly every once in a while to create a playful, scattered look. Let dry at least 1 hour.

4 Carefully peel off the washi tape to reveal the letter.

5 Apply yellow paint to the outside edge of the plaque, and let dry.

Tips

* This plaque could easily be used as part of a cute display on a bookshelf, or, if you'd like to add hardware to the back, it could be hung on a wall.
* Consider using a circle-shaped stamp or even fingerprints to create the dotted background.

Pompom Press

A cardboard template keeps those pesky, but oh-so-cute, pompoms in line for this lettering project!

Sketch one uppercase letter and one lowercase letter on a scrap piece of cardboard with a pencil, using a straight-edge or ruler to make the edges straight. Cut out each letter with a sharp craft knife, sketch in the inner shape of the letters if necessary, and then cut those parts out with a sharp craft knife, too. Cover small sections of the letters with white glue, and quickly adhere pompoms before the glue dries. Continue working your way around the letters, one short section of glue at a time, until both letters are completely covered with pompoms. Let dry.

Polka Dot ABCs

The end of a pencil eraser and watercolor paints in assorted colors are all you need to make this cute alphabet.

Sketch the entire alphabet in uppercase letters on white paper with a black marker. Hold the paper in front of a window or light box, with another piece of blank white paper over it. Dip the eraser end of a pencil into watercolor paint, and trace over the alphabet by making dots on the blank paper along the guiding lines. Re-dip the eraser as needed to finish each letter, and wipe the eraser off with a damp paper towel or rag in between each letter.

lettering lesson

Be of Good Cheer

Combine mixed media, a favorite phrase, and freeform letters in this colorful project.

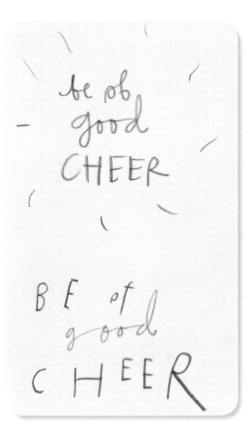

figure A

figure B

What You'll Need

* Pencil
* Scratch paper
* Translucent paper
* Square piece of white heavyweight paper
* Acrylic paint in various colors
* Paintbrush
* Collage materials, such as scraps from other paintings
* Glue
* Transfer paper
* Washi or painter's tape
* Colored pencils in blue and other assorted colors
* Alphabet rubber stamps

Method

1 With a pencil, sketch out a favorite phrase several times on a scratch piece of paper using different combinations of lettering styles, until you find a version of it that you love (fig. A).

2 Trace that favorite version of the phrase by placing a piece of translucent paper over the phrase and copying it with a pencil (fig. B).

3 Add color and texture to a square piece of paper using acrylic paints in various colors as well as collage materials using glue. Don't worry about patterns or straight lines; the messier the better! But do leave one area open so you can add your phrase in later. Let dry (fig. C).

4 Lay a piece of transfer paper down onto the dried painting over the exact area where you'd like the phrase to appear. Lay the translucent paper with the traced phrase down on top of the transfer paper, and tape both down lightly with washi or painter's tape. Trace over the words lightly enough that it doesn't ruin the painting, but firmly enough that the words transfer (fig. D).

5 Carefully remove the tape, the translucent paper, and the transfer paper from the painting.

6 Go over the traced writing with a blue colored pencil.

7 If you'd like, add another word or two using rubber stamps painted with red acrylic paint. Let dry.

8 Add in more bits of collage, more paint, and more colored pencil marks to finish your composition.

figure C

figure D

Twisted Word Play

Pipe cleaners are super kid-friendly, fun to work with, and, best of all, not permanent! You can keep twisting and playing with pipe cleaners until the projects are just right.

Write out a name or phrase in script writing on a scrap piece of paper with a black marker. Grab a stack of pipe cleaners, and start bending and manipulating one at a time to match the script writing. When you've reached the end of one pipe cleaner, simply twist it a few times with the next pipe cleaner and keep bending. Check your work every so often by laying the pipe cleaner on top of the written version of the word.

K is for Koala

It's pretty much impossible to cut out paper letters perfectly. Same thing goes for cutting animal shapes. That's a good thing because the imperfections make this project extra cute and adorable.

figure A

figure B

What You'll Need

* Green and gray pieces of paper
* Scissors
* Inside of a security envelope
* Black marker
* Pink office supply stickers
* Pencil
* White acrylic paint
* Paintbrush
* Colored pencils in assorted colors
* Gel medium
* Brush
* Collage materials, such as scraps of other paintings
* Glue

Method

1 Cut out your desired letters from pieces of green and gray paper with a pair of scissors. Focus on cutting the overall outline of the shape first, and then adding in the details that make the letter next.

2 Use the patterned paper inside of a security envelope, and sketch the shape of a koala or other desired animal on it. Practice first on a piece of plain white paper if you want to. Cut out the shape (fig. A).

3 Draw eyes, nose, and a mouth on the koala with a black marker, and add office supply stickers for the cheeks. Scribble the ear fur in with a pencil.

4 Paint a white background on a small board or canvas with a paintbrush. Let dry.

5 Doodle in the area where the koala shape will be and also add details such as polka dots, dashed lines, and straight lines on the board with colored pencils (fig. B).

6 Adhere the letters and koala shape to the board with a thin layer of gel medium and a brush.

7 Add collage materials, such as scraps of other painting projects or paper you love, to the board using glue.

Tip

Don't stop at just animals for this project—think favorite foods, colors, or activities!

Jennifer Orkin Lewis

www.augustwren.com

I think lettering projects are so fun because they give us a chance to play with something so familiar. We read, write, and see interesting signs and advertisements all around us every day. We all know how to make basic letters, so anything extra we can do to make them different or embellish them is exciting. Making my own unique and interesting versions of something familiar is really fun. Lettering is also so doable—all you need is paper and a pen!

favorite letter

I love the letter "O." It's the first letter of my last name, and I love that I can make a cute loop on the top of it. It also can turn into a face or a flower or a wheel, and it can be more round or more of an oval. There are so many possibilities!

favorite lettering instruments

I love paint, a paintbrush, and a black pen. I feel most comfortable with a paintbrush—it's like an extension of my hand. Combining my painting with a black pen sharpens it up and adds fun detail.

A Very Good Day

This project breaks down letters into simple shapes. You will love thinking of letters in terms of rectangles, ovals, and bold colors.

figure A

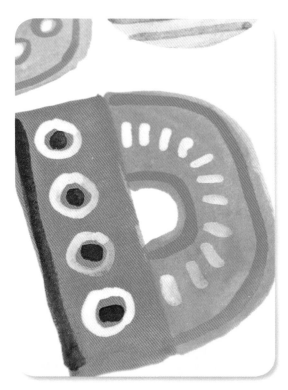

figure B

What You'll Need

* Pencil
* White paper
* Watercolor paints in assorted colors
* Paintbrush
* Water
* White acrylic paint

Method

1 Lightly sketch "A Very Good Day" in pencil on a piece of paper by breaking down each letter into rectangles or ovals that overlap. For example, sketch the "A" by drawing two overlapping rectangles with a third small overlapped rectangle shown as the triangle in the center of the letter.

2 Add color to each separate rectangle or oval shape using watercolors and a paintbrush. Within each letter, keep the colors related so each letter is still pretty simple. Let dry (fig. A).

3 Add stripes, dots, dashes, or scallops to each letter using either a darker shade of watercolor paint or white acrylic paint. Let dry (fig. B).

Tip

Imagine different ways to divide up each letter. Try working with half of a letter at a time, or think about different shapes that could overlap to make each letter.

Love, Happy, Joy

This colorful leafy garden is made up of simple uppercase
letters, flowers, and leaves.

figure A

figure B

What You'll Need

* Pencil
* White paper
* Gel pens in assorted colors
* Markers in assorted colors

Method

1 With a pencil, lightly draw uppercase letters to spell the words "Love," "Happy," and "Joy" on a white piece of paper. Focus on using thin lines to make the letters, and leave space between each letter.

2 Go back over the pencil lines with gel pens in various colors.

3 Doodle leaf shapes along each line of every letter, using markers in various colors. Play with different leaf shapes (think long and narrow or short and wide, and close together or spread apart) on each letter, but keep it simple. Slight scallops or even dashes with the marker can easily resemble leaf shapes (fig. A).

4 Add color to the inside of any enclosed portions of the letters, such as the "A," "P," and "O," using markers in assorted colors. I chose to use a solid color in some of the enclosed shapes and patterns and doodles in the rest (fig. B).

5 Doodle flower and petal shapes at the end of some of the letters as well as inside some of the letters, using gel pens in various colors.

6 Add details to the leaves such as a line down the center, using gel pens in assorted colors.

7 Using the same basic technique—starting with the gel pen line, adding leaf and flower shapes with the marker, and then adding detail with the gel pen—draw flourishes at the top and bottom of the paper.

Tip

No need to stick with leaf shapes to surround these letters. You could just as easily doodle flower shapes along each line for another version of a spring garden.

Faces in Letters

These standard block letters transform into quirky characters with just a few fun facial expressions and lots of color!

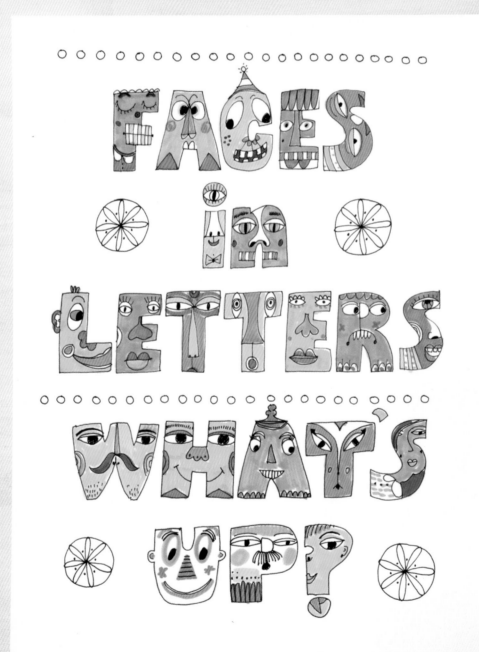

What You'll Need

* ✳ **Pencil**
* ✳ **White paper**
* ✳ **Extra fine-point black pen**
* ✳ **Thin markers in assorted colors**

Method

1. Using a pencil, lightly draw the words "Faces in Letters" and "What's Up?" in big block letters on a white piece of paper.

2. Doodle a face inside each letter by adding eyes, noses, and mouths with the pencil. Make each part of the face using simple shapes, such as "U" shapes for closed eyes, large ovals for open eyes, rectangles with stripes for mouths, and triangles for noses.

3. Personalize each character by adding cheeks, ears, and mustaches with the pencil.

4. Go back over each pencil line with an extra fine-point black pen. Let dry.

5. Add color to each character letter using thin markers in assorted colors.

6. Draw a row of tiny dots above each phrase with the extra fine-point black pen.

7. Add four flower shapes inside of circles around the outside of the phrases.

Tip

There is no end to the personality you can give these characters. Turn them all sideways, add bows to their hair and shoes on their feet, and imagine them as fairies or fishes or monsters or cartoon characters. Have fun!

Gold & White

Gel pen letters stand out against the bold black background on these motivating signs.

Lightly sketch a phrase, such as "Awesome and Very Cool" or "Awesome and Amazing" using a pencil on a piece of black paper. Experiment with different thicknesses and heights in your letters, but try to keep the style consistent within each word. Go back over the pencil marks with a white gel pen. Add white and gold color to the letters with gel pens, adding thin and thick stripes, dots, and dashes as well as solid areas. Embellish the background of the paper by doodling small stars, circles, and snowflake shapes.

Watercolor Dot ABCs

This project juxtaposes loose watercolors with linear letters, making it a great project for those who are learning how to mix colors and explore lettering styles.

Add large dots of color to a white piece of paper using watercolors in assorted colors and a paintbrush. Let each dot of color slightly overlap the next dot so the colors bleed into each other and you can see the mixed color each combination creates. Let dry, then write each uppercase letter of the alphabet and the numbers 1–10 directly in the center of each dot with an extra fine-point black pen, leaving the top row of dots empty. Add 3–4 slightly curved lines to each line of every letter and number with the extra fine-point black pen, and then add petal shapes at each end of every letter and tiny flowers in between each dot.

Jenny Sweeney

www.jennysweeneydesigns.com

From the time I was young I was taught and encouraged to create, and I experimented and used my imagination with simple, everyday items. Lettering is such an achievable, tangible way to be creative, because anyone can grab a pencil and play and doodle with letters. I never ever tire of being inspired by the simplicity of black ink on white paper, and I love the statement of beautiful, simple, and quirky lines. One of the best things about lettering is it doesn't stop at just a piece of paper and a pencil. You can letter with stamps made from potatoes or cut-out letters, and then you can use your lettering projects in so many different ways—from cards to wall hangings to gifts.

favorite letter

I very much like the letter "G."
I love the mix of curved and
straight lines, and the uppercase
version looks so much different
than the lowercase version. The
letter "G" can be strong and
classic or silly and playful. I love
drawing it to cradle and protect
other letters.

favorite lettering instruments

My favorite tools for lettering
are Japanese brush pens,
line markers, charcoal,
India ink, and beautiful,
super heavyweight paper
by French Paper or Crane's.
Add in the diversity of fun,
simple tools like markers and
scissors when I am working
on lettering, and my heart
swells with possibilities.

lettering lesson

Stamped with Love

Carving letters and shapes out of a potato creates a fun, handmade lettered look. Carve each letter and shape out carefully, and then use the final product to make heartfelt gift tags.

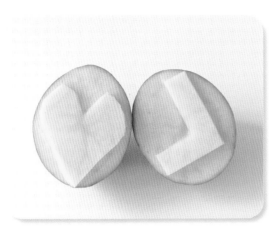

figure A

figure B

figure C

What You'll Need

* Potatoes
* Small, sharp knife
* Spoon
* Paper towel
* Acrylic paint in pink, purple, red, and yellow
* Paper plate
* Cardstock
* Scissors
* Markers in pink and blue
* Hole punch
* Dot page reinforcement stickers
* Ribbons, yarn, or pompoms

Method

1 With an adult's help, cut potatoes in half using a knife.

2 Carve out letters and shapes on the cut side of the potato using a knife. Just as with a regular stamp, you want to have the image protrude, carving away the excess around it. Scoop out larger areas with a spoon. If the potatoes have too much moisture, pat them dry occasionally in between cuts with a paper towel (fig. A).

3 Place various colors of acrylic paint on a paper plate.

4 Dip the potato stamp into the desired color, and press it firmly on a piece of cardstock (fig. B). Repeat with each letter to create the desired word (fig. C).

5 Cut the cardstock into a tag shape with scissors.

6 Trace the outside of each tag with a marker.

7 Punch a hole on the side of the tag, and apply dot reinforcement stickers to the hole on the front and back of the tag.

8 Tie a ribbon, piece of yarn, or pompom through the hole, and then adhere it to a gift.

Tip

Experiment with how saturated the color is by dipping the potatoes into the acrylic paint just partway instead of completely submersing them. This will create the more speckled and lighter look.

Cut-Out and Creative

There are several variations to these cut-out words, including cutting out an entire word or cutting out one letter at a time. Either way, these letters can be used to make signs, gift tags, or party favors, or just for fun around the house!

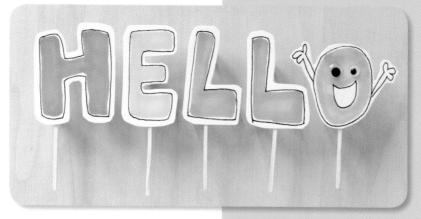

figure A

What You'll Need

* **White heavyweight paper**
* **Extra fine-point black pen**
* **Markers in blue, pink, magenta, orange, and tan**
* **Scissors**
* **Googly craft eyes**
* **Glue**
* **Toothpicks**

Method

Goober Bookmark Technique

1 Draw the outlines of letters to spell the word "Goober" on a heavyweight white piece of paper using an extra fine-point black pen.

2 Draw a frame around the entire word by sketching two imperfect lines.

3 Doodle the head and arms of a fun character in the lower right-hand corner of the frame, as if it's coming out of the frame. Add details such as eyes, a nose, and antennae.

4 Add color to the insides of the letters, the frame, and the background of the image using markers.

5 Cut around the edge of the entire frame, leaving a small white border, and then use as a bookmark.

Hello Cupcake Technique

1 Draw the outlines of letters to spell the word "Hello" on a heavyweight white piece of paper using an extra fine-point black pen.

2 Add eyes and arms to the "O" shape using an extra fine-point black pen.

3 Add color to each letter using markers.

4 Cut around the edge of each letter, leaving a small white border.

5 Adhere googly eyes to the "O" using glue.

6 Adhere each letter to a toothpick using glue, and then use as cupcake toppers.

Tip

Stick to one color palette to fit a theme, if you'd like! Even if I'm not thinking of a party theme, for example, I like to use a color palette of 3–4 colors to give all the letters a cohesive look.

Critter ABCs

Personality and character can be seen in alphabet letters, with the use of your imagination!

Draw the block outline of each letter of the alphabet and the numbers 1–9 across two pieces of white paper using an extra fine-point black pen. Add dimension to each letter by drawing an additional line to the left and below each letter and number. Create critters out of each letter by adding eyes, arms, ears, wings, feet, and whatever other details speak to you. Think closed and open eyes, straight and curved arms—even eyelashes and antennae! Add color to each letter using the markers in assorted colors.

Love and Parties

Critters can be combined with letters in myriad ways. Working with the letters in a consistent manner keeps the look clean, even while experimenting with lots of different character looks.

Sketch a row of fun characters sitting on a colored base, and add letters to each character by drawing bubbles coming out of the top of each character's head. Then, for an alternative, try sketching letters, adding frames around the letters, and then doodling fun characters coming out of the frames.

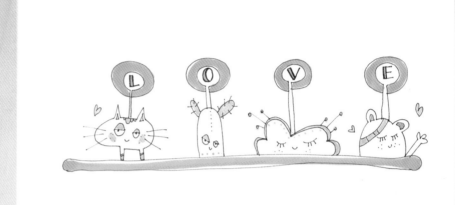

Stamped and Inked

Potato stamps are just the base of this project, and allow the doodled letters and details to really pop.

What You'll Need

* **Potatoes**
* **Small, sharp knife**
* **Spoon**
* **Paper towel**
* **Acrylic paint in pink, red, and yellow**
* **Paper plate**
* **White heavyweight paper**
* **Brush pen**
* **Black ink**

Method

1 With an adult's help, cut potatoes in half using a knife.

2 Using a knife, carve out simple shapes, such as a circle or a heart, on the cut side of the potato. Just as with a regular stamp, you want to have the image protrude, carving away the excess around it. Scoop out larger areas with a spoon. If the potatoes have too much moisture, pat them dry occasionally in between cuts with a paper towel.

3 Place various shades of pink, yellow, and red acrylic paint on a paper plate.

4 Dip the potato stamp into the desired color, and press it firmly on a piece of heavyweight white paper. Repeat with the same shape until you have one shape for each letter of the word you'd like to write.

5 Let dry.

6 Draw letters over the stamped shapes, both in outline form and script form, to spell words such as "Happy," "Birthday," or "Love," using a brush pen and black ink.

7 Add details, such as scalloped borders, dots, hearts, and characters to some of the letters using a brush pen and black ink.

Tip

The imperfect nature of the stamp mingles well with the imperfect, playful ink lines. Don't worry about the edges or lines being "perfect" for this project!

Aimee Dotich

www.artsyville.com

Mixed tapes were huge when I was a kid, and I spent entire weekends illustrating and lettering cassette covers. To this day I'm inspired by the groovy lettering on album covers and music posters from the 1960s and '70s, and I also still love filling blank pages and spaces of all kinds with letters and doodles. There's nothing worse than looking at a blank page and not knowing what to put on it, so my solution is to just start creating. I try not to overthink it, and instead I make a few random marks and shapes on my pages to then use as guides and jumping-off points to create letters and doodles.

favorite letter

My favorite letter is "A" because it's the first letter of the alphabet, the initial of my first name and my Artsyville website, and it's a powerful and versatile indefinite article.

favorite lettering instruments

My favorite lettering tools are colored pencils and black markers. Permanent black markers are wonderful for lettering, because they don't bleed through paper and they are easy to find in stores.

lettering lesson

Word Soup

This part-brainstorming, part-drawing activity is a great way to remember a special memory or event and a fun exercise in thinking up creative words.

figure A

figure B

Tips

- If you're worried about all of your words fitting in your shape, make a rough draft of the word soup shape on a scratch piece of paper. This will give you a chance to play with the placement of the words before working in colored pencil, which is hard to erase completely.

- Frame your creation and give it to a family member or friend who shared the memory with you.

What You'll Need

✳ **Scratch paper**

✳ **Pencil**

✳ **Black paper**

✳ **Colored pencils in assorted colors**

Method

1 Think of a special memory or fun event you'd like to remember. On a piece of scratch paper, write down words and short phrases that make you think of this special event.

2 On a piece of black paper, draw the outline of an object that represents this memory, such as a heart, tree, house, or flower. Try to fill as much of the black paper as you can with the outline (fig. A).

3 Add the brainstormed words to the shape using colored pencils. Utilize the entire shape by writing the words and phrases in unusual paths, curves—even upside-down! Leave a small amount of black space around each word, so you can embellish in the next step (fig. B).

4 Go back over each word and phrase with additional colors to make the words thicker and more chalkboard-like.

5 Fill in some of the letters, such as "e" and "d," with colored pencils.

6 Using colored pencils, doodle a colorful border made up of scallops and dots around the large shape.

lettering lesson

Dream Banner

Rather than drawing the alphabet in this project, you can freehand doodle any shape you'd like, and then use templates and a pair of scissors to make each letter.

figure A

figure B

What You'll Need

* Heavyweight paper in black and other assorted colors
* Colored pencils in white and other assorted colors
* Pencil
* Scissors
* Glue
* Hole punch
* Yarn

Method

1 Fill an entire piece of black paper by drawing loose spirals using colored pencils (fig. A).

2 Draw the letters "D," "R," "E," "A," and "M" on a piece of heavyweight paper with a pencil, and cut each one out around the edges to make templates. Don't worry about cutting the holes out of the "D," "R," or "A" (fig. B).

3 Using the templates you just cut out, trace each letter on the doodle-filled black paper using a white colored pencil.

4 Carefully cut out each letter from the doodle-filled black paper along the white colored pencil line (fig. C, next page).

5 Adhere each letter to a piece of bright heavyweight paper using glue. Trim around the letter so only a short edge of bright paper is left, but take care to leave enough space to punch holes on the top edge.

6 Use scraps of the bright colored paper to fill the holes on the "D," "R," and "A" (fig. D).

7 Punch two holes at the top of each letter piece, and string yarn through all of the letters.

Tip

The sky is the limit with words for this banner. Try a "Happy Birthday" banner or a banner for your name!

figure C

figure D

Shape Mash ABCs

Colored pencils, imagination, and freedom are all you need to create this playful alphabet.

Using colored pencils, draw all the letters of the alphabet on a piece of black paper. Write some uppercase letters, some lowercase letters, some letters bigger, and some letters smaller. Once the entire alphabet is on the page, make your letters bigger and bolder by going over the letters several times with the same color. Let some of the black paper show through both inside and around the border of your letters. Add different doodles and borders around each letter.

Create Plates

Drawing and personalizing each letter in this word allows for experimentation with lots of different lettering and doodling styles.

figure A

figure B

What You'll Need

* Drinking glass
* Heavyweight paper in black and red
* Colored pencils in assorted colors
* Scissors
* Glue

Method

1. Using a colored pencil, trace the bottom of a drinking glass or other round object on a piece of heavyweight black paper. Repeat this step for each letter in "Create."

2. Cut out each circle with a pair of scissors.

3. Lightly sketch one letter per circle to spell the word "Create."

4. Go over over each letter with additional layers and colors to make it look more chalk-like (fig. A).

5. Add doodles to fill each circle using colored pencils, but leave space between the letter and the start of the doodle so each letter really stands out (fig. B).

6. Adhere the circles on a piece of red heavyweight paper using glue.

Tips

* Try different shapes for this activity. Triangles, ovals, rectangles, or squares will all work nicely.

* For a different look, write out the full word on one piece of black paper, and add the colors and doodles around the entire word.

CREATE & MAKE
choose happiness
SEEK ADVENTURE
do good things

Amy Tangerine

www.amytangerine.com

I loved doodling with my friends growing up, and as early as fourth grade I remember sharing our pens and markers with one another as we passed notes. We even made notebooks for each other, and we would use them to share writing style ideas! Soon after my love of doodling began, my mom took me to Hong Kong, and I went crazy collecting pencils, marker sets, and all kinds of cute stationery items. There's something so special about a handwritten sentiment, especially since people crave that handmade touch in our digital world now more than ever. No email can match the feeling of a handwritten note.

favorite letter

My favorite letter is probably the uppercase "R." Because I don't love the way it looks in lowercase form when I write it, I typically try and do an uppercase version, which makes things look a bit quirky and fun.

favorite lettering instruments

Good pens are a vice for me. I think the right markers and pens actually motivate you to write more things down! I also like to use the back of American Crafts textured cardstock, as I'm really comfortable with the way ink flows on it.

Watercolor Brush Script

Brush script can be created using an inexpensive watercolor set and lots of practice! This project leaves space for great personal interpretation, with room to choose any phrase and any combination of colors you'd like.

positive mind.
positive vibes.
positive life.

Love·DREAM
bReathe·believe
CREATE & MAKE
choose happiness
SEEK ADVENTURE
do good things.
TRY YOUR BEST.
* always look on the brightside.

ABCDEF
GHIJKL
MNOPQ
RSTUV
WXYZ
abcdefg
hijklmno
pqrstuvwxyz

What You'll Need

* Paintbrush
* Water
* Watercolors in assorted colors
* Paper

Method

1 Dip your paintbrush in water, then your desired color.

2 Draw each letter of the alphabet, or each letter of your chosen word or phrase with the paintbrush on a white piece of paper. As you work through each letter, make each downstroke thicker than the upstrokes. Practice saying "thick" as you go down and "thin" as you go up to get in the habit.

3 To keep the watercolors looking clean and bright, rinse your paintbrush regularly in water in between colors.

4 Let dry.

Tip

Brush lettering is very on-trend right now. Look at examples of artists who write brush scripts that you like, but in the end, practice what comes naturally for you. You'll be able to add your own special twist to it as you get more comfortable.

lettering lesson
Stitched Sentiments

Get a grown-up to help you thread the needle if you need the support, and then make this very clever project.

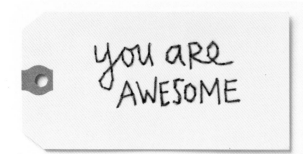

What You'll Need

* **Pencil**
* **Prefabricated tags**
* **Foam mat or mousepad**
* **Paper piercer**
* **Eraser**
* **Craft thread in dark gray**
* **Hand-sewing needle**
* **Paper**
* **Double-sided tape**

Method

1 With a pencil, lightly write out each word of the phrase "Home is wherever I am when I'm with you" on separate prefabricated tags.

2 Place each tag on a foam mat or mousepad.

3 Poke holes about ¼ inch apart on each pencil line using a paper piercer.

4 Erase the pencil marks.

5 Backstitch the letters using craft thread and a hand-sewing needle.

6 Tie knots in the back of each tag once that word is completed.

7 Adhere each tag to a piece of white heavyweight paper using double-sided tape.

Tip

These stitched words would fit perfectly on a sweet card for a loved one. Follow the same instructions, but adhere the tags to a card—or piece of paper that can be folded into a card—in the last step.

lettering lesson
Striped ABCs

This playful alphabet is made up entirely of horizontal lines. A sketched guideline of block letters ensures the final alphabet looks great, and the classic pattern leaves plenty of room to play with colors.

figure A

figure B

figure C

What You'll Need

* **Pencil**
* **Paper**
* **Extra fine-point pens in assorted colors**
* **Eraser**

Method

1 Using a pencil, lightly sketch a block version of each letter in the alphabet on a piece of paper (fig. A).

2 At the end of the alphabet, lightly draw two heart shapes with a pencil.

3 Draw horizontal lines inside each letter and heart shape with extra fine-point pens in assorted colors. The color pattern is up to you (fig. B)!

4 Let the pen ink dry completely.

5 Erase the pencil marks with an eraser (fig. C).

Tip

Because the stripe pattern is so classic, you can easily play around with the colors you decide to use. You could work in a rainbow pattern, or you could work in a random pattern. You could even limit yourself to one or two colors if you have a favorite color scheme.

Pam Garrison

www.pamgarrison.typepad.com

As a kid I was always creating and making projects, whether it was crafting with my mom or practicing my calligraphy. Lettering was then, and still is, such a simple, easy way to be creative. At the very basic end of it, all you need is a pencil and paper! Lettering can be bold and playful or soft and elegant, and the really great thing is that you can make your lettering style all your own, just like your handwriting. When I'm working on lettering projects, I always leave plenty of time and space to play and experiment, because that's when you can really make it your own.

favorite letters

I love lots of letters, but "S" and "O" are especially enjoyable to me because they have curves and can be made in a large variety of ways. And even with that variety, they are still recognizable and easy to spot.

favorite lettering instruments

One of my favorite writing instruments is an extra-fine Pilot Precise Grip pen, because it's available at many office supply stores and it has a really smooth feel to it. When I'm adding color, I love neon highlighters. The width of the highlighter tip is great for writing uppercase block letters.

lettering lesson

Sprayed and Stenciled

Adding interesting details to large block letters is a fun juxtaposition, and it allows you to play with whatever doodles you'd like in a specific space.

figure A

figure B

What You'll Need

* **Large paper stencils**
* **Paper**
* **Washi tape**
* **Ink spray in red and blue**
* **Paint pens in assorted colors**
* **Permanent markers in assorted colors**
* **Scissors**

Method

1 Adhere large paper stencils to pieces of white paper using washi tape or another easily removable tape.

2 Apply blue and red ink spray to the stencils, and let dry.

3 Carefully remove the stencils from the paper.

4 Draw and doodle on top of the letters with paint pens and permanent markers. Experiment with adding detail both strictly within the letter (fig. A), as well as outside the letter (fig. B).

5 Cut around the edge of the letter, being sure to cut around the doodles as needed.

Tip

You may want to use the ink spray and stencils on top of a protective surface, just in case the ink spray bleeds through or goes beyond the piece of white paper.

Stained Glass

Breaking up these bright neon letters with geometric lines coupled with watercolors painted inside the shapes creates a unique stained glass effect for the alphabet.

figure A

figure B

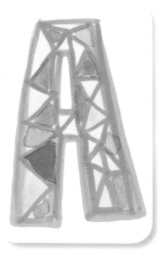

figure C

What You'll Need

* Paper
* Paint pen in neon pink
* Watercolor paints in assorted colors
* Paintbrush
* Water

Method

1   Draw the entire alphabet in large block letter forms with a neon pink paint pen (fig. A).

2   Using the same neon pink paint pen, add lines inside the block letters to mimic stained glass, using randomly placed straight lines in whatever direction you'd like (fig. B).

3   Let the paint pen markings dry.

4   Add color in between the lines in the block letters using watercolor paints and a paintbrush. Rinse the paintbrush off in water when changing colors to keep each color clear. The paint pen will act as a resist, so the watercolors will not bleed into the paint pen (fig. C).

Tip

Experiment with the shapes you use inside of the block letters. Triangles or flowers, for example, would produce a completely different look.

Double Trouble

This bold alphabet is easy to create, plus it's easy to make all your own simply by changing up the colors and types of pens you use.

On a piece of paper, draw each letter of the alphabet using large markers or poster pens. Let dry. Find a different kind of marker—perhaps a different width, different color, or different type of marker such as a chalk pen—and draw a second alphabet directly on top of, or just to the side of, the first alphabet. If your second marker creates a thinner line than the first, you could draw directly on top of the first alphabet, but if the two markers are similar in width it works better to draw the second alphabet just to the side of the first.

Wild and Free Stenciled Alphabet

Scratch paper from previous art projects, or paper decorated completely freeform, serves as the base for this bright, wild alphabet. Stenciled block letters create order from the more playful background, and then cut-out letters can be used to make a banner, sign, or gift tags.

Gather colorful, pretty scratch paper from previous art projects, or make your own! If you want to make your own, apply watercolor or acrylic paint in whatever colors you'd like to a piece of heavy white paper. Feel free to paint in a random manner. Let the paint dry, and then trace small alphabet stencils over the top of the painted sections with a fine-point black pen. Remove the stencil and add patterns, such as stripes or polka dots, to the inside of the block letters. Add detail and color to these patterns with neon highlighter markers.

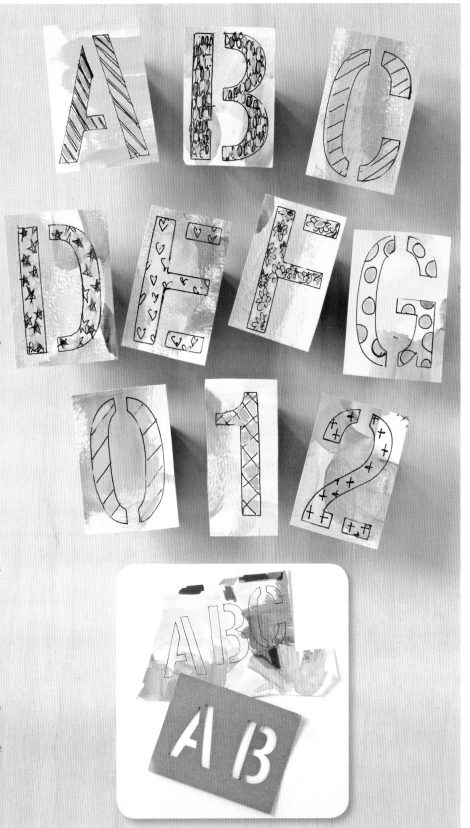

Bubbly Letters

A colorful background made up of watercolor paints serves as a great foundation for an alphabet made with gel pens. Neon-colored gel pens in particular really stand out against the rainbow of bubbles!

Fill an entire piece of paper with splotches of color using watercolor paints in assorted colors and a paintbrush, and let dry. Draw block alphabet letters on top of each colored splotch using gel pens in assorted colors. Add details, such as stripes, stars, or dots, in some of the letters using gel pens.

Claire Donovan

www.hearthandmade.co.uk

I've always loved creative journaling, sketching, and crafting, but I haven't always loved my handwriting. In fact, it wasn't until a few years ago that I decided I wanted to improve my penmanship. I researched and learned new techniques for handwriting—all the way down to how I sat and held my pencil—and I dedicated lots of time to practicing my handwriting with a pencil on graph paper. Once I felt more comfortable with my basic handwriting, I took creative lettering classes, and I completely fell in love with lettering as an art form. For anyone starting out, I'd recommend lots of repetition, experimentation, and play!

favorite letters

My favorite letter is either an uppercase "B" or "R." There are so many possibilities in moving the middle bar on those letters.

favorite lettering instruments

I can't start any lettering project without a mechanical pencil—size 0.3 is my favorite. I also always have a Pentel retractable eraser, a guided ruler, and black ink Uni Pin pens in various sizes.

Chunky Funky Alphabet

Just some colored pencils are all you need to make these chunky and funky letters.

Write all the letters of the alphabet and numbers 1-9 on a piece of white paper with colored pencils. Vary between uppercase and lowercase letters. Fill in some letters, such as "B" and "H" completely, and fill in portions of other letters, such as "T" and "L." Add dots, scallops, and lines to some of the letters, such as "D" and "M." Most of all, have fun using your ideas to make these letters reflect your inner funky and playful personality.

Name Placard

Once the cereal has been eaten, use the box to create a super fun name placard!

figure A

figure B

What You'll Need

* Ruler
* Pencil
* Scissors
* Cereal box
* Paintbrush
* White gesso
* Water
* Coral acrylic paint
* White gel pen

Method

1 Using a ruler, pencil, and scissors, mark then cut a cereal box to make a rectangle that is big enough to fit the desired name. For this project, the rectangle measured approximately 10 x 4 inches (25.4 x 10.2 cm).

2 Using a paintbrush, apply two to three coats of white gesso to the inside of the cut rectangle (fig. A). Allow the gesso to dry in between coats. Rinse brush in water.

3 Add a layer of acrylic paint to the gessoed piece using a paintbrush. Let dry. Rinse brush in water.

4 Doodle scallop edges using a pencil (fig. B), and cut along the doodle on all sides.

5 Doodle in the letters of the words with a pencil (fig. C). Start with the letter that is either the middle letter of the name or the middle two letters of the name so that the entire name becomes centered on the piece.

6 Trace over the penciled letters with a white gel pen and add dots and dashes along the scalloped edges.

Tip

There are other types of boxes that will work well, like pasta boxes and cracker boxes. They are thick enough to hold the applications of paint but pliable enough to cut fairly easily.

figure C

Beautiful Happy

Create this colorful sign and use it every day as a reminder to count the many reasons to be happy.

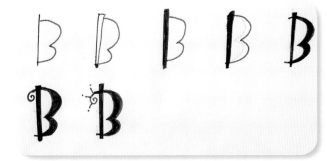

figure A

figure B

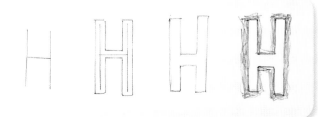

figure C

Tip

If you want to avoid making so many dots at the end, you can do steps 1 through 7 on a piece of white paper and then cut out the piece along the scalloped edges and adhere the piece onto a piece of patterned paper.

What You'll Need

* Ruler
* Pencil
* Scissors
* Cereal box
* Colored pencils in assorted colors

Method

1 Using a ruler, pencil, and scissors, mark then cut a cereal box to make a rectangle that is big enough to fit the desired text. For this project, the rectangle measured approximately 7 x 5 inches (17.8 x 12.7 cm).

2 Doodle scallop edges around the rectangle and cut along the doodle on all sides to create a template.

3 Place the template onto a piece of white paper and trace around the edge with a blue colored pencil. Go over the tracing several times to make the scallops look thicker.

4 Practice making the desired letters on a scratch piece of paper so you can plan out how big each letter should be in order to fill the space.

5 For the green letters, use lines to make simple block letters.

6 For the word "beautiful," start with simple lines and then add extra lines to thicken the letters. Fill in the space with the pencil. Add swirls to some of the start and end points (fig. A and fig. B).

7 For the word "happy," start with simple lines made lightly as guides around which you will add thicker lines to make chunkier block letters. Use the colored pencil to thicken the chunky outlines and use that same colored pencil with a lighter hand to make light and airy lines all around each letter (fig. C).

8 Use a yellow colored pencil to make small dots on the space outside of the scalloped area.

Allison Nadeau

www.inkmeetspaper.com

My first grade teacher really emphasized the importance of proper penmanship, and I remember countless exercises in forming letters and words in her class. I never saw writing as a chore though—I was the kid who loved when we got to practice handwriting. Once I had the foundation of proper letter formation, I just kept writing and exploring letter shapes and expanding on lettering styles. Over the years, I've learned that lettering really takes time. While a project may look like it was created effortlessly with its big swoops and loops, it's actually a very considerate and slow process. I often remind myself to embrace the slowness and immerse myself in the process. And the more you do it, the better you'll get!

favorite letter

I am loving drawing the uppercase letter "H" in script right now and making big swoops and loops out of the ascenders.

favorite lettering instruments

I always have a simple No. 2 pencil, a clear plastic ruler, a white Staedtler eraser, a light box, brush pens, Micron pens, and gel pens on hand to start a lettering project.

Flowery ABCs

Delicate, tiny flowers and leaves add a pretty pop of character to this lovely alphabet.

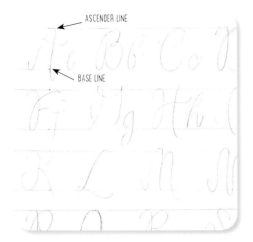

figure A

figure B

figure C

What You'll Need

* **Clear ruler**
* **Pencil**
* **White paper**
* **Fine-point black ink pen**
* **Eraser**

Method

1 Draw guidelines, including an ascender line and a base line, using a clear ruler and a pencil on a piece of paper. Leave about 1 inch (2.5 cm) between the ascender and base lines, and then leave about ½ inch (1.3 cm) between each set of lines.

2 Sketch loopy uppercase letters in the space between the ascender line and base line with a pencil. Leave about 1½ inch (3.8 cm) between each uppercase letter. Keep in mind that the guidelines are just that— guidelines—so feel free to add little tails and curls that go beyond the lines slightly (fig. A).

3 Go back and add a lowercase letter to match each uppercase letter, and then add the numbers 0–9 at the end.

4 Carefully go over the pencil lines of each letter and number with a fine-point black ink pen. Be careful not to smudge the ink with your hand. Let dry completely (fig. B).

5 Erase pencil marks with an eraser.

6 Add floral and foliage embellishments, such as petals, leaves, and tiny dots, to each letter with the fine-point black ink pen (fig. C).

Tip

If you'd like, you could add color to the leaves and flowers with colored pencils.

Birthday Greetings

This happy sign is inspired by calligraphy, but it achieves the look without nibs and with added color.

figure A

figure B

figure C

What You'll Need

* **White paper**
* **Pencil**
* **Fine-point black ink pen**
* **Eraser**
* **Colored pencils in assorted colors**

Method

1 Loosely letter the words "Happy Birthday" in a cursive-style script on a piece of paper with a pencil (fig. A).

2 Add another pencil stroke to make each down stroke appear thicker.

3 Erase any areas where one line crosses the fill of the down stroke. For example, erase the middle of the cross stroke on the "T," so the entirety of the thick down stroke is uninterrupted.

4 Carefully go back over the pencil marks with a fine-point black ink pen. Let dry completely (fig. B).

5 Erase the pencil marks with an eraser.

6 Doodle flourishes at the beginning and end of each word and in the space around the words with the fine-point black ink pen. Let dry completely (fig. C).

7 Add color to the fills of the down strokes with colored pencils.

Tip

Instead of adding one color in each down stroke, consider adding patterns, such as dots, lines, or cross-hatches.

lettering lesson
Hello Postcard

This tall and skinny lettering style is perfect for making postcards or addressing small envelopes with long addresses. It's also great practice—and super fun!

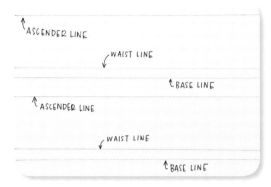

figure A

figure B

figure C

What You'll Need

* **Clear ruler**
* **Pencil**
* **White heavyweight paper, 4 x 6 inches (10.2 x 15.2 cm)**
* **Thick black pen**
* **Eraser**

Method

1 Draw two sets of guidelines, including an ascender line and a base line, using a clear ruler and a pencil on a 4 x 6-inch (10.2 x 15.2 cm) heavyweight piece of paper. Start with the top ascender line about ½ inch (1.3 cm) from the top of the paper and the bottom base line about ½ inch (1.3 cm) from the bottom of the paper. Measure 1¼ inch (3.2 cm) from the top ascender line to draw the top base line, and then measure 1¼ inch (3.2 cm) from the bottom base line to draw the bottom ascender line.

2 For each set of guidelines, draw a waist line ¼ inch (0.6 cm) up from the base line (fig. A).

3 Sketch "Hello from Charleston" using the lines as a guide. Try to make your letters as narrow as possible, and use the waist line as a guideline for letters with multiple parts, such as the "F," "R," and "A" (fig. B).

4 Doodle a tiny heart at the end of the message.

5 Go back over each letter and shape with a thick black pen. Let dry (fig. C).

6 Erase all of the pencil lines with an eraser.

Tip

If you'd like to use your own city but the city name is short, try adding the abbreviation or full name of the state.

lettering lesson

Sunshine Script

Using guidelines as a reference gives this freehand watercolor lettering a clean look.

hey sunshine!

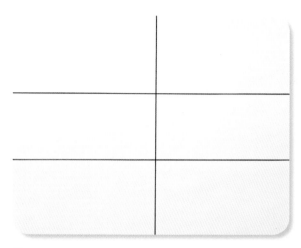

figure A

figure B

What You'll Need

* White paper
* Ruler
* Black permanent marker
* White heavyweight paper, 8 x 10 inches (20.3 x 25.4 cm)
* Paintbrush
* Water
* Watercolor paint in yellow and orange

Method

1 Draw a vertical line directly in the middle of a white piece of paper using a ruler and a black permanent marker.

2 Draw two horizontal lines on the paper, one about one-third of the way down and one about two-thirds of the way down, using a ruler and a permanent marker (fig. A).

3 Position an 8 x 10-inch (20.3 x 25.4 cm) piece of white heavyweight paper on top of the guideline sheet, taking care to center the heavyweight paper directly in the middle. You will use the guidelines that you can see through the heavyweight paper to help you as you write the words. Use the vertical line to keep the words centered and the two horizontal lines to write the two words in a straight line.

4 Dip your brush in water and then load it with yellow watercolor paint. Add a dab of orange for depth, and then begin writing "Hey Sunshine." Make the down strokes thicker and the upstrokes thinner. Add more paint to the brush as the color gets lighter. Let dry (fig. B).

Tips

* Hold the brush just as you would hold a regular pen.
* Play with the amount of water on the brush as compared to the amount of paint. How does more water affect the strength of the color?

A Roped Hello

For this project, I was inspired to make letters out of the
loops and twists of a piece of string.

figure A

figure B

figure C

What You'll Need

* **String**
* **White paper**
* **Clear tape**
* **Orange marker**
* **Pencil**
* **Eraser**
* **Fine-point black ink pen**

Method

1 Make the word "Hello" out of string by twisting and shaping it on top of a piece of white paper (fig. A).

2 Once you're satisfied with the way it looks, secure the string to the paper with clear tape.

3 Write the word "Hello" on another piece of white paper with an orange marker, mimicking the curves and loops of the string version of the word. Don't lift your marker as you work; instead, act as if the marker were a piece of connected string as well (fig. B). Check your work by occasionally laying the written version of the word on top of the string version.

4 Carefully outline the orange marker strokes with a pencil.

5 Using your eraser, erase any areas where lines cross over each other. For example, erase the middle of the cross stroke on the "L," so the front loop of the letter is uninterrupted.

6 Draw small lines within the outlines using a pencil (fig. C).

7 Go back over the pencil marks with an ink pen. Let dry completely.

8 Erase the pencil marks.

Tip

Try to keep the marker line the same thickness throughout; this will help it look even more like a piece of string.

April Meeker

www.instagram.com/secondsister

As soon as I could write I started experimenting with fun and different ways to write my name. I doodled all over my school folders and notebooks! I love creative lettering because it's not only fun to look at and read, but it also communicates further meaning. When I want to be inspired, I like to pay careful attention to my surroundings. By visiting art museums, looking at letters used on signs, and finding advertisements I like, I can find new ideas. And if I'm ever frustrated when a letter doesn't turn out exactly like I see it in my head, I remember that no photographer would ever take one photo of an event and assume it's great—sometimes you have to create multiple art pieces before you make one that you love.

favorite letter

My favorite letter is probably "Q." I like the little squiggly tail, and I like words that start with the "Q" sound.

favorite lettering instruments

I typically gravitate toward watercolors, but I'm always trying to mix it up and experiment with new mediums. Markers are easy to work with and give brilliant color, and I've recently enjoyed learning to use a calligraphy pen as well.

Critter Letters

I made this alphabet by thinking of each letter as a different critter or forest object. ABCs are so fun when you think of an "M" as a quirky fox or an "A" as an evergreen tree!

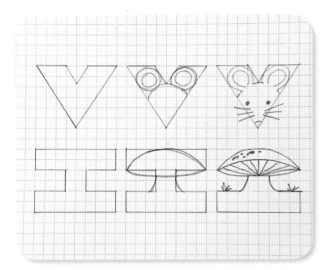

figure A

figure B

April Meeker   89

What You'll Need

* Pencil
* Graph paper
* Light source, such as a light box or window
* White paper
* Extra fine-point black pen
* Eraser
* Markers in assorted colors

Method

1   Using a pencil, sketch out letters of the alphabet on a piece of graph paper. Use the squares as a guide to make sure all of the letters are roughly the same size (fig. A).

2   Think of each letter as the outline of the shape of a woodland creature, such as a mouse, caterpillar, tree, or owl. Experiment on the graph paper by drawing different doodles and details on the letters until you're happy with each one.

3   Using a pencil, trace the final design of each letter onto a piece of white paper by holding the piece of white paper on top of the piece of graph paper, and then holding both pieces of paper in front of a light source, such as a light box or window.

4   Trace all of the pencil lines with an extra fine-point black pen, and let dry. Erase any pencil lines that are still visible.

5   Add color to each letter based on the individual designs, such as green for the trees and leaves, yellow for the caterpillar, red for the mushroom, and blue for the water and sky (fig. B).

Tip

This same approach would work with any theme, so no need to stick with woodland creatures! You could draw each letter based on a beach theme or an underwater theme, for example.

lettering lesson

Stamped with Love

Making a hand-carved stamp of a favorite phrase means you can create multiples of the same project without having to actually write the exact phrase multiple times! An entire set of cards and envelopes would make the sweetest custom stationery set.

figure A

Tip

If you don't have a blank white card, make your own! Simply fold a heavy piece of cardstock in half to match the size of your envelope.

What You'll Need

* ✳ **Pencil**
* ✳ **Square piece of paper**
* ✳ **Rubber stamp carving block**
* ✳ **Sharp craft knife or linoleum cutter**
* ✳ **Pink ink pad**
* ✳ **Scratch paper**
* ✳ **Matching white card and envelope**

Method

1   On a small square piece of paper, sketch out the letters to spell "Love" in a way that fills the square, with "L" and "O" on the top line and "V" and "E" on the bottom line. Instead of a circle for the middle of the "O," draw a small heart. Fill in the sketch completely with a pencil.

2   Flip the square piece of paper over and place it on top of a rubber stamp carving block, then transfer the mirror version of the image onto the block by rubbing the entire backside of the paper with the side of a pencil. The pencil lead used to fill in the sketch in step 1 will transfer to the rubber to serve as a guide for carving.

3   With an an adult's help, use a sharp craft knife or linoleum cutter to begin carving your eraser or block using the rubbed image as a guide. Start by carving the major outlines, and then carve the smaller details. The raised portion of the image is what's going to show up as a stamp, so make sure you pay attention to which parts of the image you're going to carve away (fig. A).

5   As you're finishing carving your stamp, adhere ink to the stamp and press it on a scratch piece of paper. This will allow you to see the stamp in action, which will point out areas that may need closer carves.

6   Once your stamp is complete, liberally ink it with a pink ink pad, and then carefully stamp the front of a white card. Let dry.

7   Carve another small heart stamp. Liberally ink the heart stamp with the ink pad, and then carefully stamp it on the outside flap of the envelope. Let dry.

Sebastian's Love Notes

This project strings together love notes with the help of Sebastian and his big ball of yarn.

figure A

figure B

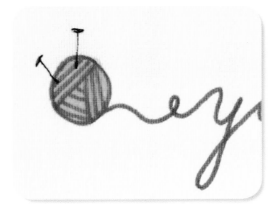

figure C

Tip

If you are making a card for someone, you might consider drawing Sebastian with their initial on the front, and then writing your message on the inside. You can copy Sebastian exactly as he is, or create your own furry friend.

What You'll Need

* **Small pieces of white and black cardstock**

* **Red extra fine-point marker**

* **Pencil**

* **Black extra fine-point pen**

* **Pink marker**

* **Glue**

Method

1 On a piece of white cardstock, write "You are my favorite" in cursive script with a red extra fine-point marker.

2 Connect all of the words in the phrase by drawing swirly lines in between each word with the red extra fine-point marker.

3 In the space to the right of the phrase, draw a small cat with a pencil by first sketching a larger oval for the body, a small circle for the head, a smaller oval for the end of the tail, and two lines connecting the tail to the body.

4 Carefully erase all of the lines inside the cat body, so just the outline remains. Add two small triangles for ears, and sketch arms, legs, and a face.

5 Shade in the cat with the pencil, and trace over the face markings with an extra fine-point black pen (fig. A).

6 Connect the red phrase to the cat by drawing curly lines in the space between the end of the phrase and the cat's ear with the red extra fine-point red marker. Draw curved lines several times around the cat as if he were tangled in the yarn, and then draw a curly line to the right of the cat for the end of the yarn (fig. B).

7 In the space to the left of the phrase, draw a small circle with a light pink marker. Outline the circle with the red extra fine-point marker, and then draw diagonal lines through the middle of the ball. Draw curly lines between the ball and the start of the phrase to connect the ball to the word "You" (fig. C).

8 Draw two straight lines with small dots at the end with an extra fine-point black pen for the knitting needles in the ball of yarn.

9 Adhere the piece of white cardstock to a slightly larger piece of black cardstock with glue.

Christine Mason Miller

www.christinemasonmiller.com

I first started playing with creative lettering ideas in middle school, and by the time I got to high school my friends were always asking me to draw the names of their favorite bands or best friends on notebooks and posters. This trend has continued for the rest of my life, and I still enjoy playing with creative lettering. I love beautiful handwriting, and am especially inspired by the gorgeous calligraphy that used to be more common—things like old hotel guest books and ledger books with entries written in elegant, detailed script make me swoon! My advice for anyone interested in working on their lettering is to practice their handwriting first—a unique, neat, and readable style of handwriting is the best tool for creative lettering.

favorite letter

My favorite letter is "G." When it comes to creative lettering, I feel the most freedom with a "G," whether uppercase or lowercase. There are all kinds of details and embellishments I can add to make it extra expressive.

favorite lettering instruments

My favorite pens are an ultra fine-point (.038 or .05) Micron or a simple PaperMate felt tip flair. I also love using colored pencils. I have a set called Progresso by Koh-I-Noor that I love; the colored lead is the entire tip. There's no wood surrounding the tip, and the pencils are really soft, so it's easy to fill in large (and small!) areas of color.

Mad for Mandalas

My inspiration for this project was a mandala design, which is created with circular, geometric patterns. I like to create mandalas by starting with a circle in the middle and then doodling swirly lines, arches, and leaf shapes from the center outward.

On a piece of paper, write your name in chunky block letters with a pencil, making sure to leave some space in between each letter. Then, lightly draw a large mandala directly over the name. Use circles, leaves, and petals to work from the center outward until the mandala is taller than the name. Carefully trace over just the letters with an extra fine-point black pen and let dry. Erase all of the mandala's pencil marks that are inside of the letters and then carefully trace over all of the lines of the mandala that are outside of the letters. Add color to the mandala and stripes to the letters with colored pencils.

Dream Lettering

Curly letters helped me write one of my favorite quotes for this project.

Write a quote on a piece of heavyweight paper with a pencil using a combination of curly letters and more basic letters. Try to create each letter with one continuous, curly line. Make the curly letters wider on each curve by adding a second line in those areas with a pencil. Carefully trace over the quote with an extra fine-point black pen and let dry. Erase any pencil marks that are still showing. Add color to the wide curves on the curly letters with various colored pencils. Doodle dots of various sizes around the quote and color in the bigger dots with colored pencils.

lettering lesson

Feather Alphabet

I love collecting feathers on my morning walks in our neighborhood, so I decided to take this inspiration from nature and create an entire alphabet using simple, diagonal lines.

figure A

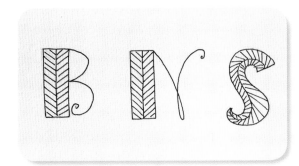

figure B

figure C

What You'll Need

✳ **White heavyweight paper**

✳ **Pencil**

✳ **Extra fine-point black pen**

✳ **Eraser**

✳ **Colored pencils in assorted colors**

Method

1 On a piece of heavyweight paper, lightly sketch out each letter of the alphabet with a pencil by first focusing on one main shape for each letter. For letters with one straight edge, such as "B," "D," and "H," draw a vertical rectangle first and then draw the curved lines to finish the letter. For letters with diagonal straight lines, such as "M," "A," and "W," draw a rectangular parallelogram before drawing the rest of the lines to finish each letter. Lastly, for the few letters with only curved lines, such as "C," "O," and "Q," draw a wide, curved shape that narrows at the end.

2 Add curly embellishments to some of the letters, like the tail on the "J" and the curl at the end of the "A" (fig. A).

3 Draw a line through the middle of each main shape and then diagonal lines coming out of that middle line to fill the shape and make it look like a feather (fig. B).

4 Carefully trace over each pencil line with an extra fine-point black pen. Let dry, and then erase any pencil marks still showing with the eraser.

5 Add color to the main shapes with assorted colored pencils. Focus on one colorway for each letter, using light and dark versions of the same color interspersed with blank white spaces (fig. C).

Tip

Use these fancy feather letters to write a friendly greeting or a cheery sign. You could doodle just the first letter of a word in feathers, or the entire phrase.

Rock Star Writing

Basic letters get the rock star treatment with this fun approach to lettering.

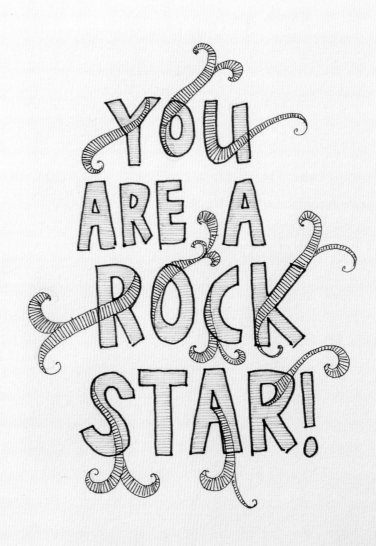

figure A

figure B

Tip

Experimenting with different embellishments is just the beginning of this project. Play around with combinations of different embellishments, and try adding color to the decorative sections as well.

What You'll Need

* Scratch paper
* Fine-point markers in black and blue
* Translucent paper
* Light source, such as a light box or window
* Pencil
* White heavyweight paper
* Eraser

Method

1 On scratch paper, draw letters "A," "B," and "C" in block letters with a fine-point black marker, leaving space in between each one (fig. A).

2 Trace the letters three separate times on three separate pieces of translucent paper by placing the translucent paper in front of the scratch piece of paper and then holding it up to a light source, such as a light box or window.

3 Experiment with various embellishments on the three different pieces of translucent paper. Follow the natural curves of each letter as you experiment with elaborate flower shapes, feather designs, and stripes (fig. B).

4 Once you've chosen your favorite design, use that approach to create a sign. With a pencil, write "You are a rock star" in block letters on a piece of heavyweight paper, and then add the embellishments of your choice in pencil just as you did on the translucent paper.

5 Carefully trace over the pencil lines with a fine-point black marker, let dry, and erase any remaining pencil lines.

6 Draw thin stripes inside each letter with a fine-point blue marker.

Lisa Solomon

www.lisasolomon.com

In a world where we are increasingly inundated with computer-generated images and type, creative lettering done by hand is something we can easily recognize and relate to. I have always been obsessed with handwriting—I remember trying to write my name in 20 different styles on blue-lined notebook paper as a young girl. I think part of my initial interest in lettering stemmed from being exposed to traditional Japanese calligraphy in my childhood. In my lettering projects now, I love to have fun and experiment. Sometimes I'll use my non-dominant hand or hold my tools in a different way just to see how it looks!

favorite letter

I don't have a favorite letter. I actually like all of them equally for different reasons.

favorite lettering instruments

I love watercolors and brushes for their unpredictability and color range. I also love Micron pens for precision and for the wide variety of weights they come in. And you can never go wrong with a pencil or a Sharpie!

lettering lesson
Schooled in Skulls

This project is a great experiment in shapes and spacing. Draw and play with several variations of the same shape, and then add letters inside those shapes for fun and quirky ABCs.

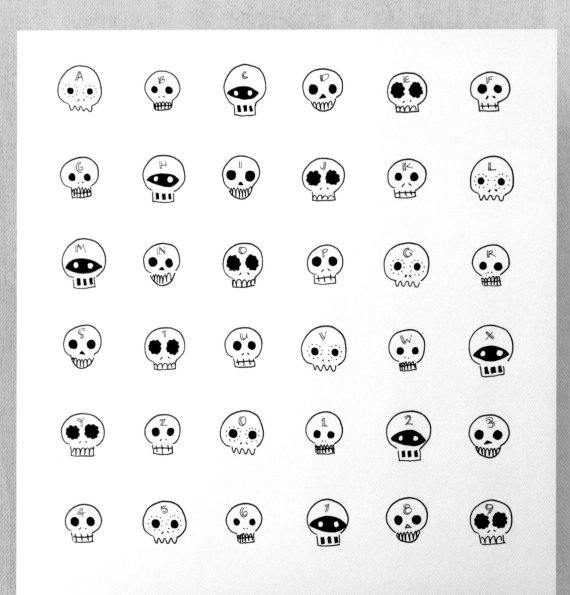

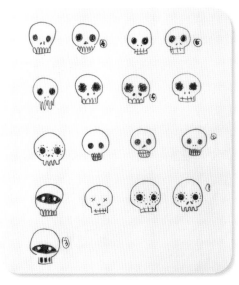

figure A

figure B

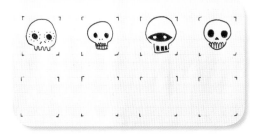

figure C

What You'll Need

* Extra fine-point black pen
* Scratch paper
* Graph paper
* White paper
* Light source, such as a light box or window

Method

1 With an extra fine-point black pen, sketch out various skull shapes on a scratch piece of paper, to brainstorm the skulls you'd like to use in your alphabet. For each skull, draw a circle, but leave a space open at the very bottom of the circle to add various mouth shapes. Think square jaws, scallops for toothy grins, rectangles to show teeth, or a combination of those for the bottom mouth portion. Experiment with eye and nose shapes as well, from triangles and straight lines for noses to flower shapes and big dots for eyes. Just be sure to leave enough space on the forehead to place the alphabet in later (fig. A).

2 Play with various alphabet styles to match the skulls on a piece of scratch paper. I ultimately decided on an uppercase alphabet, and I added one extra line to each letter for interest (fig. B).

3 Once you've decided on the skull shapes and alphabet styles you'd like to use, begin drawing the skulls on a piece of graph paper. The graph paper will allow you to space each skull out evenly and make each of them roughly the same size (fig. C). I decided to go with six different skulls staggered in a grid, so I made a grid of skulls six columns across and six rows down to complete the entire alphabet and numbers 0–9.

4 Hold another piece of paper over the graph paper in front of a light source, such as a light box or window. Trace the grid of skulls onto the paper using an extra fine-point black pen.

5 Add each alphabet letter and number to the forehead space by drawing uppercase letters with one extra line on the left side of the letter.

Tips

* You could go anywhere with this idea. Next time, try adding the alphabet inside panda shapes!
* You don't have to stick to six different skull shapes. You could really stretch your imagination and come up with 36 different shapes, or you could stick to just one shape and change up the alphabet instead.

Nature Script

This painted wreath with pretty script would be lovely framed for a gift or wall hanging.

figure A

figure B

What You'll Need

* Compass (or paper plates in different sizes)
* Thick permanent black marker
* White paper
* White heavyweight paper
* Light source, such as a light box or window
* Round watercolor brush
* Watercolor paint in orange and green
* Water
* Eraser
* Scissors

Method

1 Draw a 7-inch (17.8 cm) circle and a 9-inch (22.9 cm) circle using a compass and a thick permanent black marker on a piece of paper. You could also use a few different sizes of paper plates to make the circles if you don't have a compass (fig. A).

2 Hold another piece of heavyweight paper over the circle paper in front of a light source, such a lightbox or window.

3 Paint the decorative wreath on the heavyweight paper by doodling petal shapes with a round brush and orange watercolor paint around the entire circle, using the circle underneath as a guide.

4 Add touches of color by painting small green dots randomly in the wreath. Let dry, then erase the pencil lines.

5 Write "Let's go outside" with the round brush and green watercolors in a script style in the middle of the wreath. Let dry (fig. B).

6 Cut around the wreath so the final product is in the shape of a square.

Tip

Try writing different phrases with the watercolors, and then change the colors to match accordingly.

Janna Barrett

www.jannabarrett.com

When I feel stuck in my creative lettering projects, I like to start by drawing the alphabet. It's a good warm-up because it gets my hand used to the curves and motions, and oftentimes in the process I'll naturally start thinking of new interpretations of the letters. I've also been doodling and drawing ever since I can remember—my mom told me once there was never a page of homework that didn't come home without a drawing or doodle or lettering on the back!

favorite letter

My favorite letter is the lowercase "G" because it's so fun to draw. There seems to be more options for variation with its form because it has multiple components. Altering any little part of that letter gives a whole new attitude and character to the rest of the letters in the set.

favorite lettering instruments

When I'm sketching, I love graph paper and a mechanical pencil with soft lead. For my finished products, I love cardstock, Micron pens, and my light box to trace over sketches.

Best Buds Forever

This darling wall hanging would be the perfect gift for a dear friend.

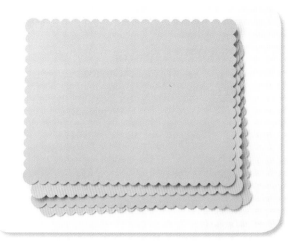

What You'll Need

* ✳ **Fine-point black marker**
* ✳ **Blue and green cardstock, one 4 x 3-inch (10.2 x 7.6 cm) piece of each color and one 5 x 4-inch (12.7 x 10.2 cm) piece of each color**
* ✳ **Glue**
* ✳ **Scallop-edged scissors**
* ✳ **White ribbon, one 2-inch (5.1 cm) piece and one 6-inch (15.2 cm) piece**
* ✳ **Strong tape**

Method

1 Outline the word "Best" in big block letters with a fine-point black marker on a 4 x 3-inch (10.2 x 7.6 cm) piece of colored cardstock. Fill in the block letters with the black marker.

2 Outline the word "Buds" in thin, curly block letters with a fine-point black marker on a 4 x 3-inch (10.2 x 7.6 cm) piece of second colored cardstock. Fill in the letters with the black marker.

3 Adhere the "Best" sign to a 5 x 4-inch (12.7 x 10.2 cm) piece of green cardstock using glue, and then adhere the "Buds" sign to a 5 x 4-inch (12.7 x 10.2 cm) piece of blue cardstock using glue. Let dry.

4 Cut around the edge of both of the larger pieces of cardstock with scallop-edged scissors.

5 Doodle dashes and dots around the edges of the larger pieces of cardstock.

6 With the "Best" sign above the "Buds" sign, turn both signs over so they are face down on a flat surface. Adhere one end of a 2-inch (5.1 cm) piece of white ribbon to the bottom of the "Best" sign using strong tape, and adhere the other end of the ribbon to the top of the "Buds" sign using strong tape.

7 Make a loop with a 6-inch (15.2 cm) piece of white ribbon, and adhere the bottom of the loop to the top of the "Best" sign using a piece of strong tape.

Tip

This would be a fun project to do with a friend. You could both write "Best Buds" in your own lettering style, then exchange one word with each other so you have a piece of your friend's writing as well. Proceed with the rest of the instructions with double the materials list, and then you'll both have a wall hanging!

Candy Shop ABCs

Sketching and experimenting with letters before tracing the final version really gave me a chance to choose my favorite versions of each letter for these fun words!

figure A

figure B

Tip

Sketching out versions of the letter before deciding which ones to trace allows you to really pick your favorites. Try approaching the shadows and details the same way—sketch various versions of the dotted and striped letters, for example, until you find your favorite. Then just trace the favorite versions for the final project.

What You'll Need

✳ **Extra fine-point black pen**

✳ **White paper**

✳ **Tracing paper**

✳ **Light source, such as a light box or window**

✳ **Fine-point markers in pink, green, yellow, purple, orange, and blue**

Method

1 With an extra fine-point black pen, sketch each letter of the alphabet in big block letters on a white piece of paper. Experiment with slightly different alterations and versions of each letter to determine your favorite.

2 Trace your favorite versions of the sketched letters on a piece of tracing paper to spell out "Candy Shop." Move the tracing paper around to find each new favorite letter before you trace it (fig. A).

3 Add lines to the outside edges of each letter to make them three-dimensional using the extra fine-point black pen. For the word "Candy," draw lines to the left and at the bottom of each letter, but don't connect the ends of each line so you have a more open, three-dimensional look. For the word "Shop," draw lines to the left and at the bottom of each letter, but draw completely connected lines on this word. Then add shadows to the bottom of each section using an extra fine-point black pen (fig. B).

4 Add straight and wavy lines and dots to the inside of the letters that spell out "Candy," using an extra fine-point black pen.

5 Hold a piece of white paper over the tracing paper in front of a light source, such as a light box or a window.

6 With an extra fine-point black pen, carefully trace the "Candy Shop" letters, including all the doodles and details, onto the piece of white paper. Let dry.

7 Add color to the inside of the letters using fine-point markers in pink, green, yellow, purple, orange, and blue.

Lemonade Stand

Hand-drawn signs for a neighborhood lemonade stand give kids and adults alike the perfect excuse to play with fun, bold lettering styles.

figure A

figure B

Tip

This same method would work to make a large poster as well. To make a large poster, sketch different parts of the word on multiple pieces of white paper, and then trace a section of the word at a time on the large poster board.

What You'll Need

* **Pencil**
* **White paper**
* **Eraser**
* **Yellow paper**
* **Light source, such as a light box or window**
* **Tape (optional)**
* **Thick black marker**
* **Fine-point black marker**

Method

1 With a pencil, write "Lemonade" and "25¢" in big block letters on a white piece of paper. Draw the words so they stretch across the entire page; you may need to erase and rework the word as you go so it fills the entire width of the paper. Leave a little space in between each letter so you can go back and add bulk to the letters in the next step (fig. A).

2 Once you are satisfied with the basic composition of the word, go back over each letter with the pencil and add bulk. Make each letter look wider by drawing over each letter multiple times to thicken it up. Try to keep the same thickness for all the letters (fig. B).

3 Hold a piece of yellow paper over the top of the white paper, in front of a light source such as a light box or window. If you're having a tricky time holding the two pieces of paper, tape the white piece of paper to the window and just hold the yellow one.

4 Trace over each letter on the yellow paper with a pencil.

5 Go back over the pencil lines with a thick black marker.

6 Add incomplete outlines to each letter using a thin black marker.

lettering lesson

Cut-Out Hello

Making stencils is a fun first step for this project. They will allow you to cut letters from any paper that then can coordinate with a background paper of your choosing.

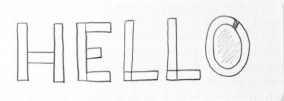

figure A

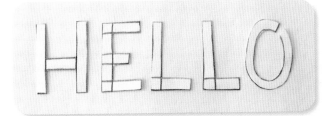

figure B

figure C

figure D

Tip

There are no limits to the words you could choose for this project. Use cheerful greetings for different holidays, or even someone's name for a thoughtful hello.

What You'll Need

* Pencil
* Heavyweight paper
* Scissors
* Gold textured paper
* White-and-gold patterned paper
* Glue

Method

1. Using a pencil, trace the word "Hello" on a piece of heavyweight paper in block, uppercase letters. Leave space in between each letter, because you will be cutting each letter out in the next step. Draw a small mark in the middle of the "O" to show where your scissors will go to cut out that empty space (fig. A).

2. Carefully cut out each letter using a pair of scissors. Remember to cut out the inside of the letter "O" (fig. B).

3. Lay your cut-out letters backwards on the back side of a gold piece of textured paper (fig. C).

4. Trace the letters on the back side of the gold paper using a pencil.

5. Carefully cut out the letters from the gold paper.

6. Lay the cut gold letters right-side up on the front side of a piece of patterned paper and decide how you would like to arrange them (fig. D).

7. One at a time, adhere the letters to the patterned paper using glue.

Spicy Labels

Made of sugar and spice and everything nice, these cute labels make standard kitchen jars extra special. Create a whole set for your mom or grandma!

Measure the existing label on a kitchen jar, and then cut a piece of white paper slightly taller and slightly wider than the existing label, as you want the new label to completely cover the existing one. Using a pencil, write the name of the spice in the center of the label with block letters. Doodle a border made of scallops and stripes on the top and bottom of the label with the pencil. Retrace over all the pencil marks with a permanent marker and let dry. Erase the pencil marks that weren't covered by the marker, then adhere the label to the jar with a piece of tape or white glue.

Jenny Doh

www.jennydoh.com

When it comes to creating art, I love to experiment. I constantly find myself switching back and forth between acrylic paint and oil paint, sketching and sewing, and even doodling and cutting. So it's no surprise that my approach to lettering projects is similar—words can be written with a simple black pen, doodled with watercolors, or even created with cut-out pieces of cardboard. In general, I tend to gravitate toward fairly simple, straightforward letters—with a dash of cleverness thrown in for fun. And more often than not, I combine my lettering with other art projects, such as stitching letters onto painted fabric or writing words on a canvas I've painted.

favorite letter

I just adore the lowercase "I." It takes up so little space, but at the same time it's unforgettable with its little dot at the top. I also like that visually it looks the same from left to right and right to left.

favorite lettering instruments

My favorite lettering tools are acrylic paint and a flat brush for their versatility, especially when used on cardboard. I also think gel highlighters are so great to add a punch of color with little effort.

Punch and Glue

The punched holes add a bubbly, friendly dimension to these words, and as a bonus—it's really fun to glue the punched holes to the paper!

Punch lots of holes from a piece of light blue paper. With a pencil, lightly write the letters of your selected word on a white piece of paper. Pick up one of the punched holes, and while holding a tiny edge of it, wipe the remaining part onto a glue stick, and then carefully adhere it to a point on the first letter. You don't need to apply glue to the entire punched hole for it to stick. Glue the next punched hole so it slightly overlaps the first one. Continue until the entire letter is covered with adhered punched holes, and then finish the entire word. Once dry, use a pick-up eraser to carefully rub and remove any stray glue marks if you see them.

Scrabble®-Inspired Alphabet

This alphabet is inspired by the cute little wooden tiles from my favorite board game: Scrabble!

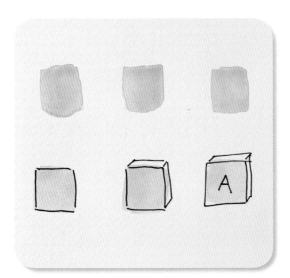

figure A

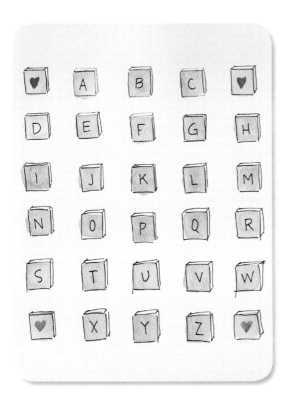

figure B

Jenny Doh 123

What You'll Need

* **Flat watercolor brush**
* **Water**
* **Light brown watercolor paint**
* **White paper**
* **Fine-point black marker**
* **Red marker**

Method

1 Load a wet watercolor brush with light brown watercolor paint.

2 Paint small squares on the paper, leaving space in between each square. Let dry.

3 Outline the squares with a fine-point black marker.

4 Make dimensional marks on the squares by adding two tiny diagonal lines at the top of the square and a tiny diagonal line at the right side of the bottom line. Make a horizontal line to connect the top diagonal lines and one vertical line to connect the side diagonals (fig. A).

5 Create simple line letters on the centers of each watercolor square.

6 On the extra squares, draw tiny hearts with a red marker (fig. B).

Tips

• Don't worry if the watercolor squares are imperfect. Actually, I think it's kind of impossible to make them into perfect squares! Once you outline them with the black marker, the imperfections will give your letters great expressiveness.

• If you prefer, you can make the squares with a light brown marker instead of watercolors.

lettering lesson
Painted and Stapled

Between painting the scrap of cardboard that serves as the base of the letters and then folding the painted scraps into letter shapes, this clever sign project is fun and different. The staples act as a quick and effective attaching mechanism and also as an unexpected design element that feels fresh and unique.

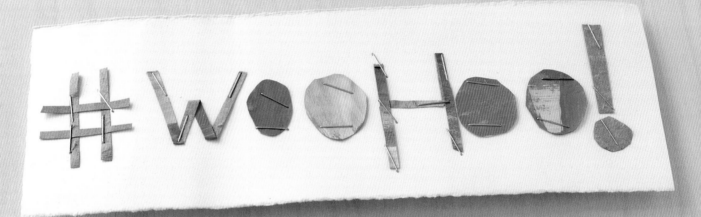

figure A

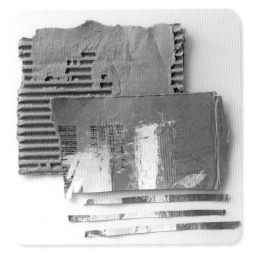

figure B

Tip

Using a rectangular piece of paper ensures that the stapler will reach any area to secure the letters, but you could easily use a different shape, like an oval or a triangle, if you'd like. Just make sure that no matter the shape, it's short enough to work with your stapler.

What You'll Need

* Acrylic paints in pink, teal, and white (or other desired colors)
* Scrap of cardboard
* Paintbrush
* White paper cut in an rectangular shape
* Stapler with staples

Method

1 Check to make sure the rectangular piece of paper is short enough for the stapler to reach all the way to the center from the top or bottom of the paper.

2 Apply a small amount of pink acrylic paint on the scrap piece of cardboard using a paintbrush. Let it dry if you don't want the next color to blend into it, or keep it slightly wet if you want the colors to slightly blend.

3 Apply a small amount of teal paint onto the cardboard, allowing it to overlap the pink paint slightly. Apply a small amount of white paint onto the cardboard, allowing it to overlap the other colors. Add more of any of these colors to fill in the cardboard with color as much as you want, letting each color dry if you don't want it to blend into the next color (fig. A).

4 Peel the painted cardboard layer from the rest of the scrap of cardboard. Don't worry if it rips in unexpected ways.

5 Cut the peeled cardboard layer into skinny strips and circles (fig. B).

6 Fold a strip in any way that works to create a letter or symbol. Sometimes the fold will need to be straight or slightly diagonal as well as forward or backward in order to create the desired letter. If one strip isn't long enough to finish each letter, add a second strip and continue folding the rest of the letter to complete each one.

7 Gather the cut-out circles for letters such as "O," or the bottom portion of an exclamation mark.

8 Carefully place the prepared letters on the rectangular piece of white paper and staple each letter in place. Make sure to staple at key folded areas to ensure the strips of paper stay in place.

Scribbled and Highlighted

All you need is a ballpoint pen and some highlighters to make letters that are awesome!

Write simple lowercase letters on a piece of white paper with a ballpoint pen. Fill in any of the enclosed spaces of the letters (for example, the middle of "A" and "B") by making an imperfect scribble with the pen. Let dry. Scribble on top of each letter using a variety of bright gel highlighters. Practice drawing a possum on scratch paper. Draw it next to the letters, and then scribble over it with highlighters. Spray the entire piece of paper with a fixative so the highlighter marks don't smear. Let dry.

Memory Game

Your friends and family will love testing their memories with this fun version of a timeless game.

Gather two small pieces of white paper for each letter of the alphabet. Use watercolors and a brush to paint a solid purple "A" on two of the paper pieces in the same style. Paint the next letter on two paper pieces in a different color and style. Do this until you have painted the entire alphabet. Let dry. Place the cards on a table with the letters facing down. Allow each player to take a turn flipping two cards over. If the player can flip a corresponding pair, they get to keep the squares. The player with the greatest number of squares at the end wins the game.

Index

ABOUT THE AUTHOR

Jenny Doh has authored numerous books, including *Washi Wonderful*, *Crochet Love*, *Craft-a-Doodle*, *Creative Lettering*, *Stamp It!*, *Journal It!*, and *We Make Dolls!* She lives in Santa Ana, California, and loves to create, stay fit, and play music. Visit *www.crescendoh.com*.